IMAGINE

THROUGH THE EYES OF...

AMAZING CREATIONS

Edited By Debbie Killingworth

First published in Great Britain in 2022 by:

Young Writers
Remus House
Coltsfoot Drive
Peterborough
PE2 9BF
Telephone: 01733 890066
Website: www.youngwriters.co.uk

Book Design by Davina Hopping

Softback ISBN 978-1-80459-263-2

Printed and bound in the UK by BookPrintingUK
Website: www.bookprintinguk.com
YB0526C

FOREWORD

WELCOME READER,

For Young Writers' latest competition Imagine, we asked primary school pupils to look beyond themselves, to think about the lives and inner thoughts of others and to put themselves in their shoes, and then write a poem about it!

Here at Young Writers our aim is to encourage creativity in children and to inspire a love of the written word, so it's great to get such an amazing response, with some absolutely fantastic poems. It's important for children to focus on and celebrate others and this competition allowed them to explore and develop their empathy, taking the time to consider the emotions and experiences of others. Whether that was their favourite celebrity, a fictional character or even their pet hamster, they rose to the challenge magnificently! The result is a collection of thoughtful and moving poems in a variety of poetic styles that also showcase their creativity and writing ability.

I'd like to congratulate all the young poets in this anthology, it's a wonderful achievement and I hope this inspires them to continue with their creative writing.

CONTENTS

St Andrews CE (A) Primary School, North Kilworth

Holly Shuff (9) 61
Florence Bell (8) 62
Eva Stanley-Blake (9) 63
Esmae O'Connell (10) 64
Olivia Wilkinson (9) 65
Natalia Stretton (8) 66
Meabh Theobald (9) 67
Oliver Lurie (10) 68
Lois Barnett (10) 69
Muneni Mukombo (9) 70
Ethan Sidorowicz (10) 71
Susie Atkinson (9) 72
Megan Stretton (9) 73
Phoebe Fielmar (9) 74
Tamara Lawrence (8) 75
Emma Davis (10) 76

St John The Baptist RC Primary School, Fauldhouse

Aaron Swan (10) 77
Caleb Farrell (10) 78
Frankie Young (9) 79
Jorga Aitchison (8) 80
Poppy Mulligan (10) 81
Noah Johnston (8) 82
Allie McLaren (10) 83
Jack Digan (9) 84
Jessica Muir (8) 85
Zofia Borowska (8) 86
Frankie McLean (7) 87
Daniel Simpson (9) 88
Bernard Brown (10) 89
Mia Davidson (10) 90
Hannah Thomson (7) 91
Jenifer Grimley (8) 92
Alix Connor (10) 93
Ava Carr (10) 94
Olivia Webster (8) 95
Johnny Shearer (7) 96
Kelcey McGarty (8) 97
Fergus Murray (8) 98
Jackson Ralston (8) 99
Emily Johnstone (7) 100
Rory Thomas (8) 101
Freddie Radbourne (7) 102
Nieve Mallon (10) 103
Shay Forrest (8) 104
Max Hilson (10) 105
Auley McDonald (8) 106

St Joseph's Primary School, Gabalfa

Jumaima Uddin (7) 107
Teddy Bowen (7) 108
Joshua Kandara (7) 109
Leo Makzal (7) 110

Strathblane Primary School, Blanefield

Phoebe Malluck (8) 111
Belle Young (9) 112
Katy Walne (10) 114
Tabitha Telling (10) 116
Sam Witherspoon (10) 118
Amelia Lowry (10) 120
Julia Kuzniarz (9) 122
Holly Busby (10) 124
Euan Faulkner (8) 126
Eilidh Hyde (10) 128
Lily Lear (10) 130
Chloe Edwards 132
Rhuari Condron (10) 134
Ollie Jackson (10) 136
Euan Orpen (8) 138
Eliza Clementine Trevithick (10) 139
Alfie Wallace (10) 140
Katie Cranna (9) 142
Jess Stevens (9) 143
Finn Malluck 144
Ailsa Symonds (9) 146
Riley Anderson (10) 147
Isla Pickard (11) 148

Wandsworth Hospital And Home Tuition PRU, London

THE POEMS

Insect

I creep along the lovely leaves
N ow all the plants are delicious and green
S lithering snakes on the forest floor below me
E ven though I can't be seen
C rawling rapidly on the ground
T unnelling under to not be found.

Eleanor Whomes (8)
Bracken Leas Primary School, Brackley

Tigers In The Moonlight

Tigers in the moonlight
As I look into the moonlight,
I see the world beside me.
I go into the cave,
I see my family,
Lying in the dazzling light of the moon,
As I walk close by,
I hear something,
I see a shadow on the wall,
I pounce out, but when I do,
It has gone.

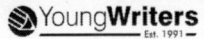

Megan Tudhope (8)
Bracken Leas Primary School, Brackley

Tigers In The Night

Tiger, tiger, burning bright
In the forest of the night
What will they hunt tonight?
Is it scrumptious fish
Or monitor lizards?
Time to sip my tea
Tiger, tiger, no more play,
Tiger, tiger, time to lie down,
Sleepy tiger, time to rest your head,
Don't make a sound.

Mia Amphlett (8)

Bracken Leas Primary School, Brackley

Surgeon

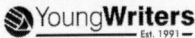

S licing my belly
U nder the bright white light
R ipping out my insides
G etting their instruments
E xtraction master
O ur heroes
N ice people helping me.

Xanthe Jones (9)
Bracken Leas Primary School, Brackley

Dentist

D rilling holes
E ntering mouths
N o more sweets
T errorising guests
I nside my body
S miling wickedly
T ickle time for me.

Ellie Inwood (9)
Bracken Leas Primary School, Brackley

Koala

A kennings poem

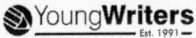

Leaf eaters
All-day sleepers
Tree climbers
Fluffy blankets
Gentle souls
Cute faces
Curious creatures.

Anna-Sophia Watermeyer (8)
Bracken Leas Primary School, Brackley

First Time To The Watering Hole

E agerly the little elephant followed her to the watering hole.
L ong, lively lines of elephants marched on to the cool, clear water.
E verywhere around little Gia appeared to be great, grey, wrinkly, immovable walls.
P anicking, Gia ran full speed towards the water's edge.
H er mother trumpeted loudly to try and warn Gia to stop.
A larmed by the sudden burst of noise, Gia tumbled into the cool, clear water with a huge splash.
N umbly she raised her head out of the water and shook her floppy ears dry.
T he long line of elephants erupted in laughter as Gia's mother's long trunk scooped her out of the water.

Isobel Stafford (10)
Oaklands Primary School, Welwyn

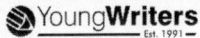

The Adventure

The wind was getting harder,
I've lost my owner.
I feel like a loner.
It's just me and the tree to fight away the thunder.
I went under the tree, safe from the thunder.
When the thunder was over, I saw a rabbit that was lost.
At the same time, I saw a wolf that was free but lost.
They ran to me when I was next to the tree
And behind it was a bee
But it was safe.
We decided to be friends and find my owner
So I wouldn't feel like a loner.
We went through the river even though we shivered.
It was just me next to the trees,
The wolf that was free and the rabbit.
We went through the forest
Until we found a man lying whilst crying.
I ran over to him to reunite.

Now it's me and the tree,
The wolf that was free,
The bunny and the man that was happy.

Amelia Buckling-Wade (8)
Oaklands Primary School, Welwyn

If I Were An Autumn Leaf

If I were an autumn leaf I could stand up high in a tree,
And I could see lots of orange leaves that look like me,
I could hear the birds tweeting in their nests,
Getting ready to go on their sunshine quest,
I could smell the cloudy bonfire smoke,
And fluffy marshmallows on sticks to poke,
I could taste the pumpkins glowing in the night,
And hear the wolves howling in the moonlight,
The children are out playing trick or treat,
While the witches and ghosts are dancing in the streets,
It is time to rest now that the bats and owls are flying around,
If I were an autumn leaf I would fall down to the ground.

Archie Doel (7)

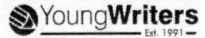

Oaklands Primary School, Welwyn

A Purrfect Day

The sun was high and the sky was blue.
There was a small butterfly that suddenly flew,
Up in the sky, up, up and away,
I looked up, but thought I would stay.
I heard a buzz behind the tree,
I woke up and thought it was bees.
I got ready to pounce,
As I looked through the grass
My eyes were bright, just like glass.
With a growling tummy, big paws and claws,
I jumped out from behind the tree and smiled with glee.
I caught my snack with my amazing jaws.
I licked my whiskers, fur and paws.
It was a purrfect day, I loved catching my prey
I choose to be a kitty every day.

Lily Philbin-Sullivan (7)
Oaklands Primary School, Welwyn

Friends

Friends are important.
You don't need to be friends with everyone
But it's worth a try.

Even if you don't end up with a friend
The journey could be fun.

Friends can just be friends or they can be best friends
Or they can even be BFFs.

Good friends are loyal.
Good friends are honest.
Good friends are kind.

Bad friends are bossy.
Bad friends are mean.
Bad friends are cruel.

So if you think you have found an honest, loyal and kind friend then be the same and keep them.
I am certain that you'll make friends.

Ava-Mae Chappell (8)
Oaklands Primary School, Welwyn

A Cow That Drives

I wanted to travel wide and far
So I escaped my farm and found a car.
I am a cow so I do not have a licence for the road
So I drove on the path, here we go!
I saw some woods in front of me
It looked like shadow monsters waving at me.
I drove through the woods and bashed every tree
When I came out there wasn't much left of me.
Suddenly my pink, neat nose smelt fish and chips
Oh I wanted to taste them on my lips.
But I am annoyed because I cannot buy any
I am a cow, I don't have money.
I will just turn around and head on home
To eat the grass all alone.

Freddie Parker (9)

Oaklands Primary School, Welwyn

Hot Chocolate

H ot chocolate is the best
O h my goodness, it beats all the rest
T remendous reactions, that's what it makes

C hocolate but warm and gooey
H ot and creamy in my mug
O n its own or with marshmallows
C ream is swirling round and round
O scar's favourite drink, which smells so nice
L ovely to have on a very cold day
A brilliant treasure, that's what it is
T rust me, you will never taste anything better
E pic drink it is, drink it up before it is too late.

Oscar O'Connell (10)
Oaklands Primary School, Welwyn

Money Honey

M en and women love this honey, a bit of sugar, it is yummy.
O ne day the man knew what to do, make some money to get some honey.
N ight has come, it's not so sunny
E very second he thought how to make money to get this honey.
Y ou might have thought this is funny.

H ow on earth can he get the money?
O n the third day he sold his spray.
N o more worry for today.
E xciting times for his women.
Y ou may think this is funny but finally the man can buy the honey.

Swazie-Mai Monaghan (10)
Oaklands Primary School, Welwyn

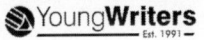

A Hot Summer's Day

I glance down at the outstanding flower fields below.
It owns so much beauty, it's you I want to show.
A waft of this amazing scent drifts up my nose,
It has daisy, tulips, lavender and rose!
There's also a plantation on the other side,
It sells cotton, corn or anything you'd like.

The tree I am perched on, a skinny branch of this bare naked tree,
This makes it unique, just like you and me!
I hear the old, wrinkly man humming an old folk song,
His face looks like a shrivelled-up prune, I can't be wrong.

Piper Brimley (10)
Oaklands Primary School, Welwyn

The Mysterious Night Sky

N ight is scary for most but it's really not so bad
I t is full of stars twinkling brightly in the dark sky
G aze up at the moon gently glowing down on you
H ow can the night be so bad?
T hese stars and moon will surely make you smile.

S nuggle into your cosy warm blanket
T ightly wrap it around your body
A nd get comfy and cuddle your teddy tight
R est is important, so tell your fears to go
S o tonight your sleep duration can flourish and grow.

Kayden Aggrey (10)
Oaklands Primary School, Welwyn

Cute Puppies

Puppies are cute, puppies are small,
Puppies are big, puppies are tall.
Everywhere you want to go puppies will be there before you know.
If you're feeling down and blue puppies will be there to comfort you.
When you need something to snuggle
Puppies will be there to give you a cuddle.
Take them for a walk every day
Puppies will just want to play and play.
Remember to feed them every day
Or they will get hungry and run away.
If they want a little nap
Take them away from any cats.
Puppies are cute!

Paige Munsie (7)
Oaklands Primary School, Welwyn

Ryan's Holiday

R eady to go, my bags are packed.
Y achts sail past in my mind.
A nd sitting at school, time goes slow.
N ow we line up.
S chool is finished, in the car, off I go.

H oliday here I come!
O ctopuses might be in the sea.
L ollies melting in the sun or...
I ce cream with a Flake, sauce and sprinkles...
D on't let the seagulls near.
A fternoons swimming, jumping in the pool.
Y ou will never get me to go home.

Ryan Borowski (8)
Oaklands Primary School, Welwyn

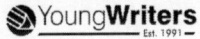

The Howling Hunter

Sharp claws but soft paws
Full moon, morning is soon
We close our eyes in the daylight
I howl and scowl and prowl and growl
Soft grey fur and yellow eyes
We eat deer and bison
I am a very good hunter
We hunt in packs
We are very fast and agile
Sometimes we kill bears
We are one of the wild dogs
We live in Arctic forests
We are in lots of fairy tales
We care about our young
We are scared of tigers and humans
We are born blind
We live for 14 to 16 years.

Kylas Setty (8)
Oaklands Primary School, Welwyn

I'm A Hungry Caterpillar Today

I am a hungry caterpillar today.
I love fruits.
I love vegetables.
All healthy food!
I like to climb green leaves.
I like to hide behind trees.
I am tired now, I'm going to sleep.
Nicely wrapped in my cosy cocoon.
Mmm, good morning world!
Wait a second, what happened to me?
I now have long beautiful wings,
Rainbow colours, smooth as silk,
I love flowers,
I love to fly over pretty trees.
What am I?

Answer: A butterfly.

Emily Lock (8)
Oaklands Primary School, Welwyn

The Wonderful World Of Vampirina

V ampirina is my name.
A nd in the dark of the night I turn into a bat.
M y awesome friends named Bridget and Poppy.
P lay with me and teach me to do human things.
I like to fly up to the full moon and dance in the light.
R eally I just like to have fun and help people.
I love my wonderful loving family who take care of me.
N ever would I hurt anyone
A nd I love my ghost, my gargoyle and Wolfie.

Summer Conder (7)
Oaklands Primary School, Welwyn

Animals

A mazing animals big and small, slim to wide, we have them all.
N ow is the time to act, time to be heroes.
I nside we all feel a mixture of sad, happy and angry but we have a duty of saving Planet Earth.
M en and ladies deforesting for wood is very wrong.
A ll of the animals are in danger, we need to act, are you with us?
L onely pets out in the world, never to be known. We are destroying Planet Earth. Please help!

Benjamin Bissmire (8)
Oaklands Primary School, Welwyn

My Mum's Wedding Day

The day arrived.
I knew straight away that this was going to be a very long day,
Yawn, yawn, yawn.
Hair, face, eyebrows, fake eyelashes,
Yawn, yawn, yawn.
Then she said, "Don't forget you are the only kid at the wedding."
Yawn, yawn, yawn.
Saying their vows, exchanging their rings,
Thousands of photographs,
Yawn, yawn, yawn.
Fabulous food, wedding cake,
Presents for being best man,
Great day!

Noah Setchell (10)
Oaklands Primary School, Welwyn

Minnow

M y name is Figels and I'm a minnow.
I like to eat small bits of soggy meat and I'm a very curious fish.
N o one likes me because I'm really clumsy.
N o one wants to eat me because I'm so small.
O n the top of the shiny cold lake under a rotted branch is where I live and hide.
W hatever I see tries to scare me because I'm easy to scare. I hate being like this but this is how I am.

Lucas Will
Oaklands Primary School, Welwyn

Cat

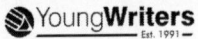

I woke up to the smell of fresh fish,
I really hoped it was in my dish.

I was eating my fish when I saw a mouse,
What was he doing in my house?
I chased that horrible mouse across the floor,
He ran under the table and right out the door.

I looked out the window and saw a bird in the tree,
She was singing a song to me.

I excitedly walked outside to have some fun,
Instead I fell asleep in the sun.

Orla McFarlane (8)

Oaklands Primary School, Welwyn

A Dog Named Lucky

There's a dog named Lucky
He's very, very fluffy
He never makes a fussy
He's a cute 'lil puppy.

He got stuck in a tree
And made friends with a bee
Who helped him to see
How to get down safe-ly.

On goes the tale of Lucky
Who also met a ducky
The duck was very clucky
Which sounds a lot like Lucky.

And that's the story of Lucky
Who's totally not sucky!

Zoe Fielder (8) & Max Fielder (10)
Oaklands Primary School, Welwyn

Foxes In The Dark

I am everywhere...
I am orange like fire with a white tail dipped in flour.
I have sharp thorns for teeth so I can kill my predator.
I am adorable but watch out... I'm fierce.
Cars drive past me quickly
My eyes glow and shimmer.
I feel scared of cars and people but I try to be brave.
I run like a wild hyena.
Behind bins I scurry to hide.
I can smell old dog bones and rotten leftovers.
I am everywhere...

Delancy Herbert (7)
Oaklands Primary School, Welwyn

Dog, Man's Best Friend

Dogs, dogs,
I love dogs,
Man's best friend,
A thief's worst fear.

Some are tiny, some are big
Some are fast, some are slow,
Some jump high some jump low,
But all are cute and cuddly.

I have a dog and his name is Robbie,
He loves running around the house,
Jumping and playing,
He is happy to welcome me
And sad to see me go.

Dogs, dogs,
I love dogs.

Kimberly Lopes (8)
Oaklands Primary School, Welwyn

Pizza, Pizza Everywhere

Bubbling cheese in your mouth.
Tomato sauce running down your throat.
My stomach, purring with delight.
Thank God Domino's delivers in the night.
Sometimes I can't have pizza so I have pasta.
Stone-baked if you like.
Dough is the best you can get.
First bite feels and tastes so nice.
In the restaurant is the best.
Bubbling cheese in your mouth.
First mouthful feels delightful.

Jacob Blacker (7)

Oaklands Primary School, Welwyn

Seaside Acrostic

S easides are fun for me because I can swim in the sea.
E els live in the sea, seals live in the sea.
A xolotls swim in the cold water of Mexico.
S and can be made into sandcastles.
I love to go to the seaside with my family.
D ouble ice cream just for me!
E nd of the day, high tide comes in and washes away the shining stones with its clear water.

William Bennett (8)
Oaklands Primary School, Welwyn

Music Is Me

Music makes me confident and happy.
Even if I was feeling bored and snappy.
What I would love to do for a living is to go on stage and just start singing.
The time I feel free is when I'm tinkling on piano keys.
I love listening to my favourite stars.
The great Shawn Mendes and Bruno Mars.
I wish I could sing all the songs they sang
Even if Mum says they're slang!

Laura-Jane Chappell (8)
Oaklands Primary School, Welwyn

Blue

When you see blue, what do you think?
Is it the colour of your bathroom sink
Or the slushy that you want to drink?

Where do you see blue?
When you are lying down in the playroom,
Imagining you're on the moon?

When do you see blue?
When you look to the sky and wonder,
And you really ponder
As you see it's blue
Then wonder, why?

Matipa Chirashe (10)
Oaklands Primary School, Welwyn

Amazing Game

They're here to stay and will never go away.
They play in red and are never in bed.
Come rain or shine they'll play just fine.
Pass and move, watch them groove.
They love scoring and are never boring.
They play all day both home and away.
They are never dozing and are always posing.
They are the best I say
So make sure you watch them play.

Samuel France (8)
Oaklands Primary School, Welwyn

The Beautiful Game

F avourite sport in the world
O ur national team makes us feel proud
O wn goals make us cry out loud
T eam Manchester United are my favourite
B est game to play with friends
A ll-time greatest player is Ronaldo
L osing a game is the worst feeling
L ove of the game is what keeps me up every night.

Alex Calderwood (10)
Oaklands Primary School, Welwyn

The Gymnast

G uide yourself to work hard.
Y ou are bold and brave, you can do anything.
M aybe just work hard and you will get there.
N ailing it can be tricky sometimes.
A wesome gymnasts do amazing twists and turns.
S ometimes things can be difficult but don't give up.
T errifically fun times are coming!

Marnie Brewster (8)
Oaklands Primary School, Welwyn

The Interesting Cheetahs

Cheetahs have shiny brown eyes.
They have a heart-shaped nose to help them sniff other animals for meat.
They can be really sneaky for meat.
They blend into the grass and jump on their prey then eat their prey.
They meow and purr.
Their cubs are playful.
They are big cats.
They're the fastest animal in the world.

Lyla Webb (8)
Oaklands Primary School, Welwyn

Unicorn

I am a unicorn,
Colourful and tall,
I have wings for flying
And a magical horn.

I am mysterious and special,
I can grant wishes too.
In any different language
I can talk to you.

I live in the forest,
I eat berries for tea,
My hair's like a rainbow,
I am a unicorn, that's me.

Harsirat Basra (7)
Oaklands Primary School, Welwyn

A Day In The Life Of Me

Wake up in the morning,
Everything is boring.
Go on games
And have mental pains.
Do a...
Get out the loo.
Ask for the swimming pool,
Go to school, where I drool.
End of the day,
Yay!
Games,
Football,
Games,
Time for bed,
Hit your head.
Go have a peep
Then I go to sleep.

Max Fielder (10)
Oaklands Primary School, Welwyn

Elephants

E lephants have big feet to step on stuff.
L ittle elephants love to play.
E lephants live in the zoo or are wild.
P owerful animals walk a long way.
H eavy and strong.
A dults look after their babies.
N aughty hunters want their tusks.
T runks that can squirt water.

Leo Smith (8)
Oaklands Primary School, Welwyn

A Day As A Cat

I am a cat sleeping in the sun,
I like to dream all day long.
I look out the window but the doorbell goes dong.
I run upstairs and hide until they are gone.
In the morning I meow for my food
And when they don't feed me I get in a mood.
I am a cat sleeping in the sun,
I like to dream all day long.

George Bailey (7)
Oaklands Primary School, Welwyn

A Day At The Beach

Welcome along to my beautiful sandy shore.
Come along and play in the wavy sea.
You will have so much fun.
Build your castle big and strong.
Everyone is welcome to come and play and enjoy your day.
Be careful in the sea, it can be cold at times.
When you go please take your belongings and litter with you.

Sophie Anderson (8)
Oaklands Primary School, Welwyn

Eco-Emergency

E arth is in danger,
M ost of it has been destroyed,
E ach and every one of us must take action,
R escue our world!
G o and make the right choice,
E very little helps,
N ever back down,
C an you help us?
Y es you, it's an eco-emergency.

Hollie Bissmire (11)
Oaklands Primary School, Welwyn

Mr Funny Boots Bones

Mr Funny Boots Bones likes to lick his toes.
His birthday is April 1st and he was dying of thirst.
Then he found some water with his daughter.
Every school needs Mr Funny Boots Bones to show them how to lick their toes.
He makes me laugh when he's in the class.
He makes me happy so then I feel chatty.

Maiya Singh (8)
Oaklands Primary School, Welwyn

Icky Wicky Caramel

Icky Wicky Caramel gets everywhere.
Sticky and slimy,
Never goes away.
In chocolate,
On pancakes,
And good for a midnight snack,
Hah hah!
Like golden syrup but a bit less sweet,
And definitely a bit less sticky icky.
Sticky and slimy,
Icky Wicky Caramel gets everywhere.

Erin Whinnett (10)
Oaklands Primary School, Welwyn

Pin The Dog

I am nine and I like cheese
I am black and fluffy
I like to roll and bite
My teddy's in the garden and on my bed
I love to smell the trees and treats Mummy and Daddy give me
After my medium walk I feel happy and tired.
I live in a giant mansion with Tim the dog and Chloe the horse.

Ben Price (8)
Oaklands Primary School, Welwyn

Something About Deniss

D riving on a stormy day
E ssex was the place that I found my pet
N ever thought to love this way
I think I will never be the same
S ee him running like the wind
S plashing puddles will always be a messy
memory of you and me.

Robin Pfeifer (8)
Oaklands Primary School, Welwyn

Life Of The Football

F lying up in the air
O ut of the keeper's hands
O n the player's head
T hrough their legs
B all in the goal
A ll the crowd cheering me on
L osing and winning is what I do
L oud noise everywhere.

Zac Antoniou (7)
Oaklands Primary School, Welwyn

Easter Bunny

E xcited to hunt for Easter eggs.
A dorable fluffy Easter bunny hopped by.
S leeping chicks in the nest.
T asty chocolate melting in the sun.
E xhausted Easter bunny from hiding all the eggs.
R osy pink spring flowers.

Ruby Croney (7)
Oaklands Primary School, Welwyn

Who Is It?

A crooked nose
Two beady eyes
A hunchback
Another set of eyes
Yellow and small
A trusty companion
A fierce hound
A grey coat
Curly, bushy hair
Bewildered and slow.
Who is it?

Answer: My neighbour and her dog.

Akaal Singh Patwal (10)
Oaklands Primary School, Welwyn

Snake

S lithers effortlessly across the tough terrain.
N imble and interesting with shiny scales.
A dded bonus is their cool beautiful colours.
K iller of rodents of all shapes and sizes.
E veryone has a place in the animal kingdom.

Charlie Penny (10)
Oaklands Primary School, Welwyn

Shadows

In the night the shadowy bright moonlight shone
over my thick orange fur and my black nose.
My big tail swished in the night as I pounced on my prey.
My prey was shrieking in the light of the night.
What am I?

Answer: I am a fox pup.

Gemma Battaglia (7)
Oaklands Primary School, Welwyn

Jonesy The Assassin

J onesy is an assassin with two pistols,
O n the rooftops, he finds his next victim.
N ever stops killing or training,
E ndless missions to fulfil.
S oon Jonesy will rule the world
Y ou won't escape Jonesy.

George Swain (10)
Oaklands Primary School, Welwyn

Tornado

I could be big or small.
I could be bigger than a skyscraper.
I could be silent or very, very noisy.
If people know I am coming they run for their lives.
I could suck things up and spit them out again
But you might never see me in your lifetime.

Max Antonel (7)
Oaklands Primary School, Welwyn

What Am I?

I am covered in fur
But I don't purr.
I have a long tail
And I am faster than a snail.
I like to dig
But I am not too big.
I am not a mouse
But I live in an underground house.
What am I?

Answer: A gerbil.

Elijah McCague (7)
Oaklands Primary School, Welwyn

Pancake Day

Pancake the hamster lives in a cage.
He has done this since a very young age.
Once he has had his food he is in a good mood.
He usually lies in his maze like a lazy hamster.
But hamsters do not eat panthers
And panthers don't eat hamsters!

Eleanor Furness (7)
Oaklands Primary School, Welwyn

The Victoria Line

V ery noisy
I am underground
C arriages have windows open
T o hear noisy wheels
O pen big doors
R ailway tracks
I go to Green Park
A t Green Park I look at the big palace.

Eliza Hebbert (8)
Oaklands Primary School, Welwyn

A Proud Peacock

I am a peacock and my name is Jake.
I strut and dance proudly, fanning my wings.
My tail blooms like a flower to get attention
And attract the females.
I feel proud when I strut.

I'm a proud peacock and my name is Jake.

Miller Watson (7)
Oaklands Primary School, Welwyn

Mr Cheetah

I'm very dangerous,
You can sometimes see me in the zoo or on a safari.

I have very sharp teeth
And black spots on my back.

I like to eat meat
And I'm the fastest animal known to mankind.

Freddie Boudier (7)
Oaklands Primary School, Welwyn

Bees

Bees have importance
The food we devour
Is made by their power
The strength bees hold
Will help us till we grow old
Daisies, lilies and even peas
Are all pollinated by bees!

Frankie Lucas (10)
Oaklands Primary School, Welwyn

Koalas

I am a cute, cuddly, calm fluffball.
I hang from trees and scrape bark.
I feast on bright, juicy eucalyptus leaves.
I live in the forests of Australia.
I hide in the tops of trees.
I am hard to find in other countries.
My habitat is hot.
I am cute to humans but I have sharp claws.
Australia is my home, it is my habitat.
I may be slow on the ground but I am quick on trees.
I am a herbivore.
My food may be poisonous to other animals and people and that is great but my habitat is full of bushes and I get bushfires all around me.
I don't have any predators around me.
We are tiny when we are babies and I can get lost which is why I stay on my mum's back until I am old enough to leave.
I have humans around me who help me when I am lost, sad or when family members aren't close to me.

Holly Shuff (9)
St Andrews CE (A) Primary School, North Kilworth

Our Home: Earth

People live on me, everyone you know is on me.
I have been around for millions of years.
I have contained many things on land and in water.
Things grow on me, things survive on me and things die on me.
People and animals feed on me.
I don't need people but people need me.
I can keep people safe and they can keep me safe and so can you.
I am everything... roads, clouds, sky and animals and oxygen.
Animals kill on me and live on me and feed on me.
I will last forever but one day you will die.
I can take care of you until you die but until then you are safe with me.
I give you fruit and vegetables but people give you meat, milk, yoghurt and cheese.
You know you're safe with me.
I gave you wood and oxygen.
This is your home... Me.

Florence Bell (8)
St Andrews CE (A) Primary School, North Kilworth

Panda And Bamboo

P andas are cute when they eat and they can climb.
A ren't they adorable when they are babies?
N ot when they become ladies.
D on't they eat bamboo? They love it more than you.
A nything they do is just cute.

B ut they aren't super smart, that doesn't matter.
A mazing as they seem
M en can adore them too.
B oring they are not.
O r are they?
O rlando, a place, they aren't really there.

C lothes are fur to them, they don't change.
U nderneath the fur is a pure heart.
T o them we are friendly.
E very day they eat bamboo.

Eva Stanley-Blake (9)
St Andrews CE (A) Primary School, North Kilworth

Mythical Creatures

I live deep in the forest, no one can see me.
I possess magical powers.
I might be a Pegasus galloping in the sky.
I might be a unicorn.
I breathe raging fire.
I fly high up in the sky.
Roar! I shriek.
I can walk on sizzling fire with no reaction.
Can you guess what I am?
I have big bulging wings coming out of my spiky back.
I shriek a roar again.
Do you have any idea what mythical creature I am now?
I like volcanos.
Boom, crash, bang! goes the volcano.
Some people say I am a myth
But I am not, I am treasure to some people.
I'm in some cultures.
I'm mysterious in many ways.

Esmae O'Connell (10)
St Andrews CE (A) Primary School, North Kilworth

The Depths Of The Deep Sea

Here we meet again in the dark, deep depths of the oceans.
Tied together by a stream of creatures.
I'm most of the planet.
Without me sea creatures are nothing.
I'm like a huge puddle of tears smushed together.
I might look happy on the outside
But on the inside I'm roaring with rage.
Whilst I am holding back my tears I have visitors.
Litter more than anything but you can't destroy me.
I have fields, water, streaming at you.
You will never destroy me,
All the plastic and pollution floats in me,
Trapping all my friends!
You will never destroy me.
I am here forever but you are not.

Olivia Wilkinson (9)
St Andrews CE (A) Primary School, North Kilworth

Spider-Man Poem

I am brave and strong.
I jump from roof to roof.
My webs are full of spiders and I jump higher than a rabbit on a trampoline.
My spiders fear humans and I fear trouble.
When trouble is around I burst in and make people fall to the ground.
I will protect the world from who knows what.
I like spiders the way people like ice cream.
I scream louder than a lion and I run like a cheetah.
If you were to see me you wouldn't see me for long because I'd be fighting crime.
Out in the suburbs of this gloomy city I will be fighting crimes and will be jumping across the moon.

Natalia Stretton (8)
St Andrews CE (A) Primary School, North Kilworth

The Life Of Nature

N obody can hurt me.
A ren't the trees so pretty?
T rees give us oxygen.
U nder the trees there is a lot of shade.
R ain falls on me.
E arth is what we live on with nature.

E veryone walks on me.
A re we safe here?
R eal animals live on me.
T ogether we will die and say goodbye.
H ow do you feel about the environment?

L ive as a team.
A nd we have amazing forests and woods.
N ow we will be careful with nature.
D o the best for nature.

Meabh Theobald (9)
St Andrews CE (A) Primary School, North Kilworth

Waves Of Rage - A Tsunami

I am rapid, raging, roaring, a force of nature.
Mighty above all!
Crash!
I carry buildings, boats and pull them down to the sea floor where it is draughty and wet and I am sure to make you drenched.
I sweep away cities and vanquish them from this world called Earth.
My force builds up due to the moon so when you're ready I'll come at you like an untamed bull.
I am the centre of the Coliseum.
I am the one who will eradicate you for the crimes you committed to the ocean. All this litter, huh! Well, it's coming back at you so be prepared.

Oliver Lurie (10)
St Andrews CE (A) Primary School, North Kilworth

The Mysteries Of The Ocean

I am a deep, dark, dangerous water world.
I am home to many fierce, fighting fish.
I am the source of all running water.
Without me, things that live in me would be a pile of bones.
I am a big puddle of tears, constantly crying.
I used to be a friend to people but now I'm not.
They litter me with plastic and pollution, it seems to fly into me.
Some of the worst storms occur upon me.
I can be as angry as a raging bull.
You can throw things into me and hurt me but I will recover.
You can't tame me but I can tame you.

Lois Barnett (10)
St Andrews CE (A) Primary School, North Kilworth

Panda

I am black and white, soft and I feast on bamboo.
I live in a rainforest but have no family that is alive.
I do not have any predators around me but I only have the insects to share the space with.
My loneliness consumes me and as the days go by I grow angrier and angrier.
You may look at me and think I'm cute and harmless but on the inside I am raging with anger.
I am slow and weak and have no good place to sleep so I sleep on the hard, rocky ground.
So I sleep there all alone because the rainforest, yes the rainforest, is my home.

Muneni Mukombo (9)
St Andrews CE (A) Primary School, North Kilworth

A Football's POV

I'm black and white, hard or soft.
I glide in the air then, *bang!*
I hit a bush and I slowly get flat like the life is getting sucked out of me.
Out of nowhere someone comes with a kit and uses it on me.
And he kicks me!
And I get pushed by a keeper.
If I could move they would be begging for mercy on their knees.
I thought I would be staying in the shop chilling until these lunatics come and buy me.
Why does it have to be me?

Ethan Sidorowicz (10)
St Andrews CE (A) Primary School, North Kilworth

The Monkey

I am small and eat bananas.
I love to play and swing on vines.
I fear bigger predators that hunt me down.
My family hunt for bananas every day.
People put me in a zoo and I escape.

Monkeys like to climb.
Monkeys like to eat.
If you want to see me, go to a zoo.
My family likes to run around everywhere.

Monkeys are furry and brown.
Some monkeys are small and some are bigger.

I'm a monkey.

Susie Atkinson (9)
St Andrews CE (A) Primary School, North Kilworth

Demogorgons

My predators fear me
I fear fire
I'm not a lion or a tiger
I have a skeleton body and I have a head like a flower
My leader made me who I am
I'm not a skeleton nor a flower.

Others think I'm bad at heart
But I have no choice
I wish I could be free like I was centuries ago
I'm just controlled
I'm not what people think of me.

Yes, I am a demogorgon.

Megan Stretton (9)
St Andrews CE (A) Primary School, North Kilworth

Nature

People walk and play on me
My waves crash into others, creating beautiful scenes
Sometimes I make disasters on my land and people
I don't mean to harm people
Some people climb on me
I rotate on Earth every day
People swim in me
Fish and species live on me
Sometimes my boulders fall, I don't want them to
I don't need people but people need me
My name is nature.

Phoebe Fielmar (9)
St Andrews CE (A) Primary School, North Kilworth

Nature

No one can hurt me
People need me but I don't need people
People climb me but I don't care
Lots of things grow on me
I'm always there
I'm everywhere
People play on me
People can play with me
People can build with me
I can make a forest with lovely animals everywhere
God has made me
No one can make me disappear.

Tamara Lawrence (8)
St Andrews CE (A) Primary School, North Kilworth

Dolphins

I am dark blue and majestic.
I am beautiful and intelligent.
I live in the underwater realm.
You might think I'm happy
But the disgusting, horrible plastic that you use hurts me.

Emma Davis (10)
St Andrews CE (A) Primary School, North Kilworth

The Big Red Planet

I am just a big hot red planet, you see,
Bouncing, rolling and shining with glee.
I look to my left and my right,
And I see my friends using all their might.

I sit there orbiting the big blue sea,
Always wondering what I could be.
I sit there using all my might,
Giving all the humans their delight.

I spin every day getting dizzy,
So every time I drink, it always gets fizzy.
I am always in the sky spinning around,
Hoping one day I will fall to the ground.

Aaron Swan (10)
St John The Baptist RC Primary School, Fauldhouse

The Creepy Ghost

I creep into your halls,
Haunting your house,
Scaring the little ones,
I create havoc so you panic.

The window opens on its own,
You're scared and creeped out,
Until I appear, you scream in terror
And make an error.

When your house is haunted,
Stay away from everyone, they could be possessed,
Like your mum, dad, brother, sister,
Even your pet.

Oops, you slipped and fell,
Well, now you're dead, that's the end.

Caleb Farrell (10)
St John The Baptist RC Primary School, Fauldhouse

Halloween

H azel, a young girl, was lost in the woods
A strange man offered her a candy apple
L ost, it was getting dark and she had no food
L ost still, she ate the apple
"O uch!" she shouted loudly in pain
"W e will help you," a still voice said
"E ek! We were lonely before we met you."
"E ee, we're coming!"
"N o, don't come. He is coming back soon."

Frankie Young (9)
St John The Baptist RC Primary School, Fauldhouse

Leaves

L eaves are really colourful in autumn
E very autumn, leaves fall off the trees
A s they fall off the trees, it is really cold
V ery often, squirrels run about
E very autumn, some squirrels make nests
S ometimes the squirrels hunt for food.

Jorga Aitchison (8)
St John The Baptist RC Primary School, Fauldhouse

What Am I?

You need to be tall, strong and able to catch a ball.
I have four people in front of three poles and it's called the goalposts.
I save the ball in the goal with four friendly, fit and healthy people defending.
What am I?

Answer: A goalkeeper.

Poppy Mulligan (10)
St John The Baptist RC Primary School, Fauldhouse

Autumn

A corns are collected to play with
U nderground, animals are ready to feast and
T rees are colourful below the branches
U nderwater life is frozen
M ore blankets are needed in bed
N ights get longer and longer.

Noah Johnston (8)
St John The Baptist RC Primary School, Fauldhouse

Sharks

S harp, shining teeth that can bite really hard
H ammerhead sharks
A ll sharks are in the sea to survive
R ound and smooth bodies like a beach ball
K iller creatures
S o many different types of sharks.

Allie McLaren (10)
St John The Baptist RC Primary School, Fauldhouse

Scotland

S nowy in November
C hilly already, don't be surprised
O ctober is a spooky month
T ea everywhere here
L ittle country
A nd little space
N oisy areas
D ays are cold or warm.

Jack Digan (9)
St John The Baptist RC Primary School, Fauldhouse

Autumn

A corns falling from the trees
U p in the sky, rain is falling
T rees' leaves are changing colour
U nderground, animals are hibernating
M aking big piles of colourful leaves
N o more sunny days.

Jessica Muir (8)
St John The Baptist RC Primary School, Fauldhouse

Autumn

A lways colourful outside in autumn
U nder trees are brown leaves
T he wind tumbles the leaves away
U nder trees are tons of colourful leaves
M any colours coming out
N o more summer for now.

Zofia Borowska (8)
St John The Baptist RC Primary School, Fauldhouse

Squirrels

S quirrels running everywhere
Q uickly up the trees and
U nder the leaves
I love squirrels, they are
R eally cute
R oaming around
E verywhere
L iving happily.

Frankie McLean (7)
St John The Baptist RC Primary School, Fauldhouse

Husky

H urry little husky, find a home
U nhappy little husky all alone
S ad little husky has no friends
K ind little seal wants to be friends together
Y ou know a friend will be there forever.

Daniel Simpson (9)
St John The Baptist RC Primary School, Fauldhouse

Halloween

H aunted house
A scary witch
L ong nights
L ate parties
O nly zombies
W itch's house
E vil skeleton
E normous cemetery
N oisy bangs!

Bernard Brown (10)
St John The Baptist RC Primary School, Fauldhouse

My Hamster

A kennings poem

Food lover
Chubby monster
Cotton ball
Sharp teeth
Night hunter
Mummy's baby
Scaredy-cat
Apple boy
Carrot lover
Finger biter
Loud scratcher
Water liker
Furry baby.

Mia Davidson (10)
St John The Baptist RC Primary School, Fauldhouse

Acorns

A pples falling
C olours all around
O ctober is when they come out
R ed, yellow and orange leaves fall from the trees
N o more hot days
S ummer days are no more.

Hannah Thomson (7)
St John The Baptist RC Primary School, Fauldhouse

Acorns

A corns falling off trees
C olourful leaves all around
O range pumpkins growing
R olling around
N o more hot days any more
S o many leaves flying around.

Jenifer Grimley (8)
St John The Baptist RC Primary School, Fauldhouse

My Pony

A kennings poem

Black-brown
Fluffy monster
Treat lover
Bath hater
Jump lover
Loud cougher
Loud snoozer
Whisker beater
Hoof kicker
Snot maker
Food gobbler
Loud feet.

Alix Connor (10)
St John The Baptist RC Primary School, Fauldhouse

My Dog, Orla

Light blonde
Cute, adorable
Big puppy
Crazy pup
Fast, speedy
Chicken lover
Funny dog
Loves playing
Loves walks
Loves toys
Adores family
Loves Gran.

Ava Carr (10)
St John The Baptist RC Primary School, Fauldhouse

Leaf

L eaves fall down from the sky
E very day, leaves are under my feet
A ll the time, I feel the leaves
F alling everywhere. Suddenly, we don't get hot weather.

Olivia Webster (8)
St John The Baptist RC Primary School, Fauldhouse

Acorns

A corns falling
C ome out in autumn and
O ctober
R attle around the trees
N othing scares them
S ome acorns are light and dark coloured.

Johnny Shearer (7)
St John The Baptist RC Primary School, Fauldhouse

Autumn

A pples falling and
U nder my feet are leaves
T umbling altogether
U nderground and
M any colours all around
N o more summer days.

Kelcey McGarty (8)
St John The Baptist RC Primary School, Fauldhouse

Autumn

A pples fall
U mbrellas are pretty
T rees are bare
U nderground, hedgehogs are hibernating
M oon shining bright
N o more hot days.

Fergus Murray (8)
St John The Baptist RC Primary School, Fauldhouse

Autumn

A pples falling
U mber leaves
T umbling to the ground
U nder my feet are leaves
M any colours are beautiful
N o more hot days.

Jackson Ralston (8)
St John The Baptist RC Primary School, Fauldhouse

Autumn

A corns
U nder my feet
T he leaves fall off the trees
U mbrellas are used in the rain
M uddy paths
N ice and cosy colours.

Emily Johnstone (7)
St John The Baptist RC Primary School, Fauldhouse

Autumn

A pples fall
U nder my feet
T rees are bare
U mbrellas are used in the rain
M any rain clouds
N o more sun.

Rory Thomas (8)
St John The Baptist RC Primary School, Fauldhouse

Trees

T he colour changes on the
R ed leaves
E verywhere there are leaves
E very tree is bare
S ummer is over.

Freddie Radbourne (7)
St John The Baptist RC Primary School, Fauldhouse

Halloween

Hairy werewolf
Caramel apples
Scary costume
Nice costume
Yummy treat
Fun party
Be safe
Be alarmed
Of the scares!

Nieve Mallon (10)
St John The Baptist RC Primary School, Fauldhouse

Trees

T rees are big
R ocks all around
E nd of autumn
E very tree is colourful
S easons are different.

Shay Forrest (8)

St John The Baptist RC Primary School, Fauldhouse

Life

L earning all the time
I nformation helps me
F ootball training
E lectric scooters are fun!

Max Hilson (10)
St John The Baptist RC Primary School, Fauldhouse

Leaf

L ittle and
E xciting little things
A ll over the forest and
F un to kick about.

Auley McDonald (8)
St John The Baptist RC Primary School, Fauldhouse

Marshmallow

M arshmallows, my favourite thing is you.
A ssorted colours, so much to choose.
R oasted by the campfire, what a treat.
S oft and spongy like a cloud.
H aving it with hot chocolate is my thing.
M elts in your mouth like a dream.
A irey, to float in your dairy.
L ight and fluffy, could be a bed for a fairy.
L icence to thrill the party.
O h my sweet, you are a delightful sweet.
W ow! Marshmallows and ice cream, my favourite
thing. Look forward to you after din-din!

Jumaima Uddin (7)
St Joseph's Primary School, Gabalfa

The Adventures Of Percy Cat

There is a neighbourhood cat called Percy
Who loves to go into the shop.
His fur is fluffy and ginger
And he drinks all the customers' pop.
They don't tell him off
Because he is so cute
He just lies in the doorway and doesn't give a hoot.
On one occasion
Percy wasn't so shy
When he jumped into a lady's car
And ate her corn beef pie.
He's scruffy and cheeky
And could do with a comb
But he makes me feel happy
When he walks past my home.

Teddy Bowen (7)
St Joseph's Primary School, Gabalfa

My Ferrari F12

F ast and furious, gliding on the track.
E legantly cruising on the charcoal-looking roads.
R ace, race and race. My Ferrari wins every race.
R evs like thunder and accelerates like lightning.
A ll day every day I take my Ferrari out to race.
R oaring like a lion, my Ferrari can be heard from miles away.
I love my Ferrari so much. Do you want a Ferrari like mine?

Joshua Kandara (7)
St Joseph's Primary School, Gabalfa

Jungle World

In the jungle lived a leopard who wanted to love.
He was kind and generous and full of life.
His pride did not like him, they thought he was dim.
However, the leopard wanted to live.
So the leopard moved on and met a chimp
Who was in trouble and started walking with a limp.
He helped the chimp to recover.
This was found out by his mother
Who was proud of him in all ways.

Leo Makzal (7)
St Joseph's Primary School, Gabalfa

Panda

I'm a panda looking for bamboo.
I feel soft like a small panda toy.
I am as playful as a kitty running through the grass.
My excited face lives in the zoo.
I'm as tired as a fluffy sloth and I sleep a lot.
I am black and white, eating bamboo.
I am a panda waiting, waiting for children.
My eyes shine bright, looking for bamboo!
I am brave like a baby joining a new family.
My body shines like a star shining down at the ground.
My fluffy face is as fluffy as a kitty.
My cuteness crushes people's hearts.
I hide when I get scared.
My body feels like a cushion lying on a cloud.
My body glows like a diamond shining down at the sun.

I am brave like a puppy meeting its new home.

Phoebe Malluck (8)
Strathblane Primary School, Blanefield

Our Planet (Reverse Poem)

All the trees will be cut down
And I'm not going to believe
All the animals in the rainforest can survive
We all need to protect the rainforest
Is not true
Rainforest destruction is a good thing
In the future, I will tell the world that
I have my priorities straight because
Creating new buildings
Is way more important than
Nature
I'll tell you something
The natural Earth flourishes
But this will not be true in my lifetime
Our Earth will suffer
A lot of people tell me that
All the trees will be cut down
I will not tell you that
Nature is beautiful

In the future or maybe even now
Coral reefs will continue to die away
No longer can it be said that
The coral reefs can be protected
It will be obvious that
The polar ice caps will keep melting
It is no good to believe that
The planet will be saved.

Now, read the poem in reverse.

Belle Young (9)
Strathblane Primary School, Blanefield

Our Earth

We will kill the forests
I will not believe that
We will stop destroying the trees
This might come as a surprise, but
Our trees keep us alive
This is not true
There are other supplies of oxygen
I will send a message to the world
My priorities are straight
Our advanced technology
Overrules the importance of
Nature and animals
Our world is full of trees
But this won't be true in the future
We will keep destroying our tree population
Naturalists tell me
Our tree numbers are dropping
I do not think
We will stop chopping them down
In my lifetime
There will be no forests

It can't be said anymore that
Our world is 'a green Earth'
It is obvious that
Our world will be more of 'a brown Earth'.
It is very foolish to believe that
We can save our mistakes.

Now read the poem in reverse, starting at the bottom.

Katy Walne (10)
Strathblane Primary School, Blanefield

Wildcats

Wildcats will become extinct
And I will never believe that
Deforestation will stop
This could shock you
Hunters will give up
Will never be true
Wildcats never had a chance to live
Soon I will share to the world the fact that
I know what I am saying
Killing
Matters more than
Living
There's a time
When wildcats roam free of hunters' influence
That will never happen
Wildcats have no future
Wildcats will go extinct
I will never conclude that
The highlands of Scotland will be alive again
In the years to come
Nobody will know of the great Scottish wildcats

No one will say
'Everyone loves wildcats'
It will become clear that
Wildcats must die because
It is not true that
Wildcats are amazing.

Now read the poem in reverse from the bottom line.

Tabitha Telling (10)

Strathblane Primary School, Blanefield

Nature On Earth (Reverse Poem)

Nature on Earth is disintegrating
And I refuse to believe that
We have a chance to save our precious world
I realise, in this lifetime
Destruction
Is more important than
Happiness
I tell you this: a shock
Polar ice caps will stop melting
Is a lie
Life won't be fixed
In the future, I will say
Life was beauty
But this will not be true in my lifetime
Plastic will wipe out our oceans
Experts tell me
Nature's beauty is being erased
I do not conclude that
Nature will survive

In the future
Destruction is unstoppable
No longer can it be said that
Every little thing makes a difference
It will be obvious that
We are monsters
It is foolish to presume that
Together we can stop this.

Now read the poem in reverse, starting at the bottom line.

Sam Witherspoon (10)
Strathblane Primary School, Blanefield

Rhinos

Rhinos are not pretty
And I refuse to believe that
Rhinos are truly beautiful inside and out
I realise this may be a huge surprise
Rhinos are actually important to us
Is a fake tale,
Rhinos are already being looked after properly
In the future I tell you this
I have my head in the right place
People having land
Is more important than
Rhinos having their home
I will state this to you
Rhinos will be safe and happy living animals
But this will not be truthful in my lifetime
They are slowly fading away
Experts tell me
Rhinos will be gone before you know it
I do not conclude that
Rhinos deserve to not be extinct
In the future,

There are too many rhinos and that is the end
No longer can it be true
Rhinos are just so rare and brilliant
It will be normal that
Rhinos are just hideous animals with huge horns
It is absolutely idiotic to think that

Rhinos are the most outstanding grey animals

Now read this in reverse

Amelia Lowry (10)
Strathblane Primary School, Blanefield

Orangutans

I hate orangutans
And I refuse to believe that
They learn everything they need to know from their mum
I realise this may be a shock, but
They are intelligent animals
Now that is a lie
They're not friendly
In the future, I will tell the world that
I know the priorities because
Destruction to make way for more buildings
Is more important than
Orangutans' happiness
So I'll tell you this:
Orangutans are very smart that they build nets to sleep in
But this will not be true in my lifetime
It is too late to save the orangutans
Experts tell me
Orangutans just take over the rainforest
I do not conclude that

They don't mind eating with their feet
In the future
Orangutans are horrible
No longer can it be said that
Some are so smart that they can use tools
It will be obvious that
Orangutans are taking over the forest
It is foolish to presume that

Baby orangutans are cute

Now read it in reverse.

Julia Kuzniarz (9)

Strathblane Primary School, Blanefield

Coral Reefs

I hate coral reefs!
And I will never believe that
We can help all them recover
This might be a shock, but
Coral reefs are homes to many creatures
Is a lie
Coral reefs can all die down
In the future, I will tell everyone alive that
Throwing rubbish in the ocean is our future
We should focus on this and not
Healthy marine life
I tell you this:
Everybody needs the existence of coral reefs
But this will never be true in my lifetime
It's too late to save the coral reefs
Experts tell me
Coral reefs don't bring life
I do not conclude that
Coral reefs will be so important
In some time,
Coral reefs will all die down

No longer can it be said that
One billion people need coral reefs as a way to survive
It's quite obvious that
Coral reefs are the dumbest things in the whole ocean
And it is foolish to presume that
Coral reefs have a great purpose.

Now read this in reverse.

Holly Busby (10)
Strathblane Primary School, Blanefield

Arctic Fox

I am a fox
White in winter, red in summer
I hunt in the day and fish at night
Devouring food as soon as I catch it
Burrowing deep in the snow
Eating rabbits, fish and even baby seals
Sleeping for an hour at most
It's hard to survive here in the Arctic
I am cute, fluffy, adorable
Sleeping...
Waiting...
Snow storms are common up here
Sheltering is hard under the snow
I wish I was in a warm place
I am so, so sad
Sleeping... *Zzzzz*
Snoring...
I am really, really cold
I need a warm place to sleep
There's not enough food.

Hunting...
Although when none of that's happening
I kind of like it up here
Until the big flying things come, build houses on my burrow!
And then they brought wolves here!
Hiding...
From predator to prey
Life has changed
People hunt me
Me!

Euan Faulkner (8)
Strathblane Primary School, Blanefield

Trees (Reverse Poem)

I hate trees
And I will not accept that
Trees give peace to the souls of mankind
People know that
We are only alive because of trees
Is not true
Trees are pointless
In heavens above, I will tell the earth that
I am always right because
Demolition to make way for roads and houses
Is always more important than
Trees
I announce
People can't survive without trees
But this will not be true in my lifetime
The leaves clog all the drains
People tell me
They drip on you when it is wet
I come to a conclusion that
We should stop chopping down trees
Is false

In the future,
We will have no trees
It will no longer be said
Trees are the key to life
It is so obvious that
Trees are never going to last
It is wrong to believe that
We will stop climate change.

Now read it in reverse.

Eilidh Hyde (10)

Strathblane Primary School, Blanefield

Coral Reefs

All the coral reefs will turn grey
And I won't believe
They will heal
You might not know this but,
The coral will flourish
Is not true
All the creatures in it will die
Soon I will tell the world that
I won't change my mind because
Selfish pleasure
Will overtake
Saving the coral
If humans will be good
It might make a come-back already
But it will not now
The coral will die
Everyone tells me
It will all turn grey
I do not think
It can all possibly be beautiful again
In the future,

Nothing will live
It is false that
Everything will be happy
It is true that
It will all be full of death and destruction
It is wrong to think that

It will be fine, and the coral will survive.

Now read it in reverse

Lily Lear (10)
Strathblane Primary School, Blanefield

Red Pandas (Reverse Poem)

Red pandas do not deserve life
And I refuse to believe that
They will always be here
I realise this may be strange, but
Red pandas are adorable
Isn't true
They are ugly beasts
I have my priorities set because
Technology
Is more important than
Saving animals
I state this:
Red pandas thrived once
But this will not be true in my children's lifetime
They will die out
Professors tell me
My children will never see them
I do not conclude that
We can save them

In the future
They will be history
No longer can it be said that
They deserve to live on Earth
It is clear that
They were not meant to be
It is stupid to presume that

We can still give red pandas life.

Now read the poem in reverse, starting at the bottom.

Chloe Edwards
Strathblane Primary School, Blanefield

Tigers (Reverse Poem)

Tigers are ugly
And I won't believe
That they will survive
It doesn't surprise me
That some people don't like them
It is a lie
That this will change
In the future, I will tell the world that
I know what I'm talking about because
Horrible
Is more important than
Excellent
I tell you this:
I know that this will change
But this will not be true in my lifetime
They will be no more
I do not conclude that
They will survive
In the future,
They'll be forgotten
No longer can it be said that

Their future will be safe
It will be obvious that
Tigers are not popular
It is foolish to presume that
Tigers are magical.

Now read it in reverse.

Rhuari Condron (10)
Strathblane Primary School, Blanefield

Coral Reefs

The coral reefs will keep breaking down
And I refuse to believe that
It will stand
I realise this may be a shock, but
There is hope
Is a lie
Ocean beauty will disappear
In the future, I will tell the world that
I know what's going on because
People
Are more important than
Animals
I tell you this:
The coral stands strong and proud
But this will not be true in my lifetime
It is dying
Experts tell me
There will be none left
I do not conclude that
It shall thrive
In the future

Nothing can change
No longer can it be said that
It will live
It will be obvious that
There is no hope
It is foolish to presume that

Coral reefs can survive

Read the poem from bottom to top.

Ollie Jackson (10)
Strathblane Primary School, Blanefield

Lionel Messi

As I run down the pitch I feel the connection with the ball.
I score top bins, gooooaaaal!
I make the goalkeeper look silly when I score.
I nutmeg every player who tries to tackle me.
When I score I blow a kiss to the crowd.
My skills are just too good.
Do you want to try and tackle me though?
Hahahahahahahahaha! Bad idea.
I make my skills look impossible.
My mates are Mbappé, Neymar and Ronaldo.
I am as good as Pelé.
My brain is ginormous.
I score all day long at my home stadium.
I make my skills look neat, as neat as the neatest writing.
I control the greatest game of football.
I have too many skills.
I feel the emotion running through my body.

We footballers are just too good!

Euan Orpen (8)
Strathblane Primary School, Blanefield

A Cowboy's Battle

Riding on a warpath, heading straight to battle,
We've abandoned hurling lassoes, and herding sleepy cattle.

What will lie at the end of this corner,
An army or a single warrior?

As we rounded the corner, our horses gasping for air,
We found a whole army assembled there.

Their faces sneering, their shouts echoing across the glen,
How, in the world were we to defeat them?

Our pistols sounded fierce and loud,
But their enormous guns made a horrible sound.

Several of our army died,
While we tried not to listen to their dreadful last cries.

Surprisingly, at the end, we defeated them,
So we went back to tending our cows once again.

Eliza Clementine Trevithick (10)
Strathblane Primary School, Blanefield

Things Aren't Always What They Seem

Slowly walking it doesn't feel it, but May will soon begin
Sand blowing slowly showing less and less as the sand absorbs the land
Drained of all my joy, all the fun is gone
That makes me annoyed!
Empty house, not even a mouse?
A man appears and shivers of fear go over the empty town
He slithers for his gun so I tell my horse, "Run boy, run!"
It felt slow motion, my mind felt like it was in the ocean
I focussed and there was nothing except us, not even the debris of dust
I know I must start counting down
He started to slither as I started to shiver
And I start 3... 2... 1... draw...

I drew my gun knowing this was not going to be fun
And then he ran away from here in absolute fear.

Alfie Wallace (10)

Strathblane Primary School, Blanefield

I Am A Coral Reef

I swish and I flow elegantly beneath the waves
overlapping the sand around.
Kind, loving fish, sealife galore and there's still
more to explore.
There's a rainbow of colours.
Daisy-yellow, poppy-red, rose-pink, baby-blue.
You should come under and I'll explore with you!
I am under the depths of the crystal-clear water
where the clownfish laugh and the turtles dash.
When the sun beams down directly on me, I feel a
warmth glowing through the sea.
Spiky seashells looking at me,
I feel so free under the sea.
I sway with the waves pushing at me,
Like the leaves on a tree swaying in the breeze.
Come under with me and you will see,
You really do feel so free!

Katie Cranna (9)
Strathblane Primary School, Blanefield

A Monster's Life

Scaly, lots of claws,
Loads of spikes trailing down my back, tail and head.
Feared around the world but on the inside I'm not that scary.
Wishing to make friends with the creatures on Planet Earth.
As many people hate me there is always at least one person that makes friends.
Those people know how monsters like me are hated.
I am quite lonely but I will always keep on trying to be less scary.
A great home and a loving family is all I want!
But there is one other downside to being a monster,
That is people want my spikes and scales,
They have magic in them.

I hope in the future people will understand the pain monsters have to go through.

Jess Stevens (9)
Strathblane Primary School, Blanefield

Rainforests

The rainforest will keep being cut back
And I'm not going to believe that
It will grow back
And this might be a bit of an impact statement but
We can save the rainforest
Is a big lie
It will never be saved
In times to come I will tell everybody that
Hate
Is always more powerful than
Love
I will say this
This rainforest could grow back
This will never happen in my life
The rainforest is doomed
But no more can it be said that
It is very nice and beautiful
It is easy to see that
It will never be as beautiful as it was and
It is wrong to think

The rainforest can survive

Now read it in reverse

Finn Malluck
Strathblane Primary School, Blanefield

Personality Of Words

Give me a word, any word,
And I will turn it into a sentence only a great poet can read.
It could be about anything,
A tree, an elephant, a bead.
I may be a thing, but I can transform
Into anything of your imagination.
You could find me in a book, or a person's words,
Hearing it, your mind will be full of concentration.
You can make me long and short,
Or rhyming, if you can.
Maybe make me realistic,
My writer usually has lots of fans.
Give me a word, any word,
And I will make it a sentence only a great reader can read.
But in every way,
I'm happy to be me.
What am I?

Answer: A poem.

Ailsa Symonds (9)
Strathblane Primary School, Blanefield

No Man's Land

Being bitten by a rattlesnake rarely comes by
Though the slithering deadly snakes can be very sly
My horse, Randy, is so fast he is hard to see
When I shout his name he comes running back to me
Walking around with my revolver in my hand
While Randy rests on the blazing hot sand
The name I've been given is Cowboy Roy
People often say I'm the most feared cowboy
The desert as always feels extremely long
For this is no place for anyone to belong
Just my horse and I galloped along the way
A cowboy is the loneliest job they say
My whole team died long ago
As my horse gets tired we go very slow.

Riley Anderson (10)
Strathblane Primary School, Blanefield

My Cowgirl Life

M y name is Cowgirl Mable,
Y oung, bold and able,

C antering along on my horse,
O ld she is, but still robust, of course,
W ith the name of Courageous Keva,
G alloping along in the heat, will not give her a fever,
I mplying the fact that I am brave,
R attlesnakes will find me my grave,
L oving the desert that I roam,

L ooking high and low to find a home,
I n my days, I herd cattle,
F earing the fact they might battle,
E vening brings the coldest nights, living in the desert has its sights!

Isla Pickard (11)
Strathblane Primary School, Blanefield

The Lone Cowboy

Riding swiftly through the tough sand,
All I can see is miles of land,
The dust in my eyes, and the heat on my chest,
On my way travelling west,
In the silence that surrounds,
I have a feeling that someone's around,
My horse rears up as it goes in the river,
I'm getting impatient, my horse starts to shiver,
My horse should get rest and so should I,
Drifting off to sleep, staring at the sky,
This is no place for anyone,
For my horse and I, it's no fun,
Where now? I wonder, we seem to have no destination,
To take a break and rest is an enormous temptation.

Josie McCleary (11)
Strathblane Primary School, Blanefield

Cairngorms

The Cairngorms should be hated
And I refuse to believe that
They are beautiful
This may be a shock but
They are a safe haven for wildlife
Is a lie
The Cairngorms are not needed
Hate
Is more important than
Hope
I tell you this:
They help wildlife to thrive
Is a lie
The Cairngorms will have gone
No longer can it be said that
This place is amazing and wild
It will be obvious that
They will be destroyed
It is foolish to presume that

The Cairngorms will remain a nice place.

Now read this from the bottom in reverse

Islay Selmes (10)

Strathblane Primary School, Blanefield

Lost In The Desert

I was sliding down a sand dune
Everybody thinking I am a loon
Just because I wanted to cross a desert that's haunted
Standing in the middle of nowhere
Just because it was a dare
Look over there, there is a horse
I guarantee its ride will be nothing like a Porsche
But it's worth a try, I think I should ride it
So I jump on its back and try to commit
But it doesn't work and I get flung to the ground
My head is spinning as I try to turn round
My face in the dirt, my body all sore
I don't see the point in trying anymore.

Ollie Goodier (11)
Strathblane Primary School, Blanefield

Tree

I sway in the wind and I patiently watch the seasons change throughout the many years.
My long arms are brown, my leaves are yellow, red, orange and green.
I am tall too, very tall, I even have a nice, pretty view.
I am curious about all the things I see but I am also happy because I am a tree.
Little bugs and lots of birds live inside of me.
They even eat me too,
I just don't know what to do!
When night comes I'm still awake,
Gazing up high seeing the glow stars make.
My hopes and dreams are to finally one day leap and lean.

Mia Battersby (8)
Strathblane Primary School, Blanefield

Banana

I wait in a bowl till someone comes and eats me.
Together me and my friends make a great bunch.
I sit around in a bowl until someone comes and peels me.
I'm yellow and brown.
When I get peeled I will be very happy.
But when I don't I will be annoyed.
I'm bored when I sit in my bowl all day.
I'm sad when nobody notices me.
When I see another banana get eaten I feel sad.
I'm bigger than the other bananas.

Finally one day I got eaten
Then I realised getting eaten isn't that fun!

Jessica Nicoll (8)
Strathblane Primary School, Blanefield

It's A Cowboy's Life For Me

Going across the desert the sun in my face
Trying to be patient with my horse's slow pace
Over sand dunes and ditches we ride along
While in my head I'm singing a song
But the Wild West is cruel and long
So no place for a child to belong
But that's our job and here's our game
We inflict on people who steal from us all the pain
But we're going over the never-ending plains
Moving the buffalo, it's all the same
As we eventually go over the top
I hear a loud boom and my heart goes stop.

James Gordon (10)
Strathblane Primary School, Blanefield

In The Wild West

Walking along the hot, hot sand
From afar, I could see some land
The sun was blaring in my boiling face
As I started to pick up the pace
I jumped on my horse and we galloped away
I knew I was not getting home today
Across the desert my horse and I
Raced away into the blue, blue sky
Jessie my horse was as tired as can be
As she slowly fell onto her knee
The temperature dropped from 40 degrees to 3.9
As it turned into bedtime
I could feel my body shutting down
As I lay on the brown, brown ground.

Jessica Conway (11)
Strathblane Primary School, Blanefield

The Wild West

T he name of I, is cowgirl Jane
H ere I live in the desert, very plain
E rrid is the name of my horse

W ith her might and power, she is the head of my force
I n the blazing hot desert I roam
L onging to find a place to call home
D esert nights are extremely cold

W hile to live here you need to be bold
E nraged cattle that I herd
S elling to traders, they get transferred
T hat is my life in the desert, it is the best but takes some effort!

Ellie Sinclair (11)
Strathblane Primary School, Blanefield

Shadow

I am a shadow,
I am alone.
I block out the sun,
Therefore the smiles.
I look into my tree's branches.
Then down at me.
In autumn,
The tree sells the most beautiful shades of red, yellow, orange the world has ever seen.
Skipping past the seasons,
Stopping at spring.
He trades the most precious gems that smell like the heart of love.
Look at me.
I am a shadow, I am alone.
A misty, bleak, grey shadow
Stares back at me.

A shadow I am, a shadow I'll be.

Florence Trevithick (9)

Strathblane Primary School, Blanefield

Cowboy Chaos

My name is Cowboy Chaos, courageous and brave all the same
I ride with my saddle and Stetson in the scorching sun
Revolver in hand, riding the right way
The Wild West is a barbarian wasteland
Riding on Black Beast, uncontrollably wild
Rotten robbers will rot with the devil
My buffalo are only the best because there are few left
If someone tries to hunt me they'll end up horrifically hanged
Robbing banks and stealing riches and rings
I'm the bravest, best and biggest cowboy in the West.

Archie Wakefield (10)
Strathblane Primary School, Blanefield

Pandas (Reverse Poem)

Pandas are the worst things ever
I certainly don't believe that
Pandas are great
It is feasible that
Pandas are stinky
It is a massive lie that
Pandas are so cute
I know
Pandas are the height of ugliness
It is unthinkable that
Pandas are so furry and nice
I will tell you this
Pandas are stupid
It is foolish to presume that
Pandas are so cool and happy.

(Now read the poem in reverse, starting at the bottom line.)

Aidan Furniss (10)
Strathblane Primary School, Blanefield

Ant And Dec

I love being in BGT!
The contestants are as funny as can be.
My left-hand man and partner in crime,
It's Dec of course, since 1989.
Saturday night is the best night of the week
As everyone loves a takeaway treat!
I'm sometimes a movie star on Saturday Night Takeaway.
As much as I like it, it's really not my forte!
Have you seen me in the jungle with the celebrities?
I love the bush tucker trials, where they eat all the beasties.

Harry Comaskey (9)
Strathblane Primary School, Blanefield

Black Crow

Galloping through the scorching, scorched sand land
Sand blinding my eye
Wind whistling across the sky
As we go over a dune tall and high
Listening to a sky-high shrill cry
A cry of a cackling crow
Fear grows everywhere I go
My horse, Black, the fastest horse around
The dark green cacti dotted on the ground
Herding cattle is what I do
The desert is the most dangerous place I knew
My name is Black Crow and there is no fiercer cowboy around.

Kasper Greve (11)
Strathblane Primary School, Blanefield

Whale

I huddle up in big groups.
I swim as slow as a sloth.
My skin is as blue as a sapphire.
I'm as hungry as ten people.
I'm happy playing in the sea.
Down in the deep blue sea you hear me singing.
I'm grateful like the wind.
My belly is as white as snow.
When people catch me I get mad.
I love to eat shrimp.
I'm as bumpy as a rock.
I am happy in the sea.

I'm the biggest animal in the world.

Katherine Wakefield (7)
Strathblane Primary School, Blanefield

Mbappé

I am as quick as a Lamborghini.
I score goals like a machine.
I am the best footballer in the world like Pelé was.
I am as cool as a mansion.
I am as precious as a hundred million.
I am bringing joy to the world.
My spirit is determined to go to the top.
My goals are as good as perfect.
When I kick the football it goes 99mph.
My shots sting for so long that it swells up.
I feel sad when I lose the Champions League.

Archie MacKinnon (8)
Strathblane Primary School, Blanefield

Cat

Adventurous.
Endangered.
I live in the forest in a wooden tent.
This is my favourite place ever!
I'm mysterious and adventurous
I am brown, black and white.
I love sleeping, eating, drinking and being on an adventure.
My stomach always aches because I only eat twice a week.
I am a cat.
I want to be found because I am lost.
Someone save me.
"Save me," I say,

"Save me, please!"

Emily Anderson (8)
Strathblane Primary School, Blanefield

Wolf

Waiting,
Waiting for prey to come.
Hungry, I might eat you.
Be careful when I'm around.
Pouncing,
Pouncing on my prey...
I have found food for myself today.
Found myself a family
That I have to protect.

Grey and strong is what I look like.
I also have very fluffy fur.

I feel brave, voracious and happy all at the same time.

The reason why is that I have found a wolf's purpose.

Mazzy McCallum (8)
Strathblane Primary School, Blanefield

Me As A Cloud

Being a cloud is ever so fun, dancing all day and gazing all night.
As wind pushes and pulls me, I fall and turn into a misty fog.
I float over land changing form.
Going over ponds and getting larger.
I fly over and under my fellow clouds, whilst staying warm in my sheep-like coat.
As I levitate above, the sun sets into a beautiful pink sky.
As night falls I rain down, disappearing into the sparkling waters of Scotland's lochs.

Nairn Sinclair (9)
Strathblane Primary School, Blanefield

Sand Cat

I am a cat, as yellow as sand.
Running over the soft floor of heat.
Leaving not a trace behind.
Not a single creature knows where my food is hidden,
Under the blazing sun my small shadow,
Hidden,
Happily jumping over the cactuses under the sunlight.
At night my ears guide me around,
Jumping, leaping, I prowl around the desert.
Then I go back to my bed,
Waiting...

For morning to come once again.

Bethany Ingham-Ayres (7)
Strathblane Primary School, Blanefield

Cowboys

I'm a cowboy riding on the dusty, dusty sand
Cattle ranching on the wide land
Riding through the big Wild West
Before my horse has a rest
Riding and running all day
Trying to find a safe place to stay
Getting up and ready to go
Off to catch the buffalo
My horse is named Betty, she likes to run
As we trot the adventure has just begun
When we ride into the distance
I feel better in an instant.

Louisa Nicoll (11)
Strathblane Primary School, Blanefield

Pandas (Reverse Poem)

I hate pandas
It is not true that
They are so cute
Somehow I believe
There are too many of them in the world.
It is a scam that
They look good how they are
They have bad habits
It is impossible that
You can be happy with them
I tell you this
They have claws and they're dangerous
It is silly to think that
Pandas are intelligent animals.

Now read in reverse.

Shona Walker (10)
Strathblane Primary School, Blanefield

Lionel Messi

I make the goalkeeper look silly.
I make a good connection with the ball.
Fast feet.
Do you think you can get the ball off me?
Hahahaha, bad idea!
I nutmeg all my opponents.
I run as fast as a cheetah.
No one can catch me.
When I get the ball I always score a goooaaal!
I always win lots of trophies.
I make my skills look so neat.

I am the best football player ever to be known.

Edward McGonagle (8)
Strathblane Primary School, Blanefield

Rubber

I eat pencil marks left from pencils.
Live in huge bundles of rubbers!
I am excited to go on another adventure.

I feel like I'm getting ignored
Because I rubbed and rubbed all day.
I'm black, and grey.

Black for my darkness, grey for my sorrow.
I just want to move but I never got the day!
I just want to move so I will keep trying and trying
And eventually, I will do it.

Noah Sutherland (8)
Strathblane Primary School, Blanefield

Dwayne 'The Rock' Johnson

Flaming tattoos burning past my chest.
One punch then you're fading into Heaven.
I explode with fiery flames zooming around the galaxy.
I feel hot and intelligent like Matilda.
I am a mighty diamond rock found deep in the underground.
In a heartbeat you open your eyes and you're in a better place.
My veins are bursting out of every one of my organs.

Can you defeat the mighty Rock?

Edward MacMillan (9)
Strathblane Primary School, Blanefield

The Race

I run like lightning, soil bursting beneath my feet.
My heart is pounding, my feet are galloping.

Determined, running a race.
Stubborn, I will not stop.
Proud, because I have won.

I run along the track, as fast as an aeroplane.
My blur trails behind me as I run.

I hunt day and night, waiting for my next meal.
Deer are my favourite.

I am happy to be me.

Lilla Gordon (8)
Strathblane Primary School, Blanefield

Star-Gazing

I am a star throughout all galaxies
I will shine in the darkened night sky
I feel happy being with others
Planets orbit me at their own speed
Sometimes I'm shooting, sometimes I'm not
I'm brave at night, shining bright
I'm a huge breath of fire
I'm bigger than the sun but from your angle, I'm not
But when I fade I turn into a black abyss.

Harris Cowan (9)
Strathblane Primary School, Blanefield

The Desert

I, Cowboy Chloe, confidently rode my horse
Deserted and dusty over the desert
Scorching, sunny, sandy desert
Riding across rapid rivers
Anxious, alone although I have a horse
Galloping gracefully near glistening rocks
Rosie my horse, rarely racing
My brown, bold and beautiful horse
My gun glows and glimmers in the sun
At night cold, calm campers try to sleep.

Charlotte Melville (11)
Strathblane Primary School, Blanefield

Cowgirls Of The Wild West

I'm called Cowgirl Catherine
I'm fierce, fabulous and fun
Every day I'm on my horse galloping ever more east
Whistling wind blows my hair making it wave wildly behind me
The cruel endless desert constantly making me crazy
My horse, Brony, all black and brown, tough as a brick wall
Running rapidly over rivers and plains
As the scorching sun shines overhead.

Sophie Armstrong (11)
Strathblane Primary School, Blanefield

Football

I am a football.
I can fly and I can sprint.
Lots of people love me.
Half of me has gotten kicked.
I love being a football.
I am a silly football.
I am in the Champions League.
No ball is better than me.
No, not that football that Americans play with.
The one where you hold the ball.

I got kicked so hard that I went back to 2012.

Kian Mills (8)
Strathblane Primary School, Blanefield

Bin

I am a bin.
Yes, a bin.
I want someone to feed me
Please, please feed me!
Blue is my colour.
A radiant blue!
Feeling excited, lazy and full
Because people notice me.
I clean up
But now I am fed up!
I have been fed so now I am calm.
Happy, full, excited and lazy
For I am a tiny blue bin!

Altogether, I feel great!

Maisie Adam (8)
Strathblane Primary School, Blanefield

Atlantic Ocean

Fresh, bitter, salty breeze makes me feel free.
As I dance, the fish play.
It is always a fun day.
Whispering wind blows,
Dark blue sky,
Stars twinkle upon me at night.
White rocks sparkle, shine, glisten,
Floating around so beautiful and calm.
Crash! Bang! Disasters came,
Angels live on in me,
I am the Atlantic Ocean.

Nulaith Mills (9)
Strathblane Primary School, Blanefield

First Launch

My rocket blasts and blows,
There are lots of controls.
I am an astronaut,
That's all I ever want to be.
When it launches, then I feel relaxed
Like sleeping on a chair.
I have a helmet I can't live without in space.
Finally, I'm in space with all the stars, space
And light I'll ever need.

Callum McKee (8)
Strathblane Primary School, Blanefield

Wolf

I am grey and I hunt my prey.
Running, jumping,
Making all the noise through the dark night.
Yes, you guessed it,
I am a wolf.
I have razor-sharp teeth.
When I see an animal, I jump at it
But it always runs away.
Then I get sad
Because I don't get fed.
And my favourite meal is deer.

Max Button (8)
Strathblane Primary School, Blanefield

Book

I love my job
I sit on a shelf
Waiting
Waiting for a child
"Read me!" I say
"Read me! Read me!"
My pages flick
Children read me
I feel amazing
Excited to be read
I feel so big
Especially compared to the others
I love being read!

I love my job.

Aria McAllister (8)
Strathblane Primary School, Blanefield

The Mystery Of The Missing Whale

Down from the deep, mysterious blue sea,
I am a big blue whale,
I am a mystery,
Same colour as the skies
With bright blue eyes.

I am a good, sweet whale
But as slow as a snail,
I am the big blue whale of the sea,
My body is as clear as can be.

The waves unfold a mystery.

Willow Lear (8)
Strathblane Primary School, Blanefield

Lego

When I see my family being used in creations
I feel more bored and jealous than ever before.
I feel a churn of desperation boiling in my body,
My beautiful colours go to waste.
I dream of being part of beautiful creations, like my brothers and sisters.

Will I ever be loved like my family?

Sam Busby (8)
Strathblane Primary School, Blanefield

Orca

I am an orca swimming gracefully.
I am as soft as silk.
And I am as wet as rain.
I live in groups.
I hunt for seals, penguins and fish.
I am black and white, swimming above the sea.
I can't wait for a child to see my amazing trick.

I am happy in the sea.

Blake Boyce (8)
Strathblane Primary School, Blanefield

I Am A Shooting Star

I am a shooting star.
I glow till I fall.
I end my life in a beautiful way.
We are a great sight for humans to look at in the dark
But we don't go away in the morning,
Our glory stays.
We are well away from Earth's surface
But it's a beautiful sight.

Charlotte Johnson (9)
Strathblane Primary School, Blanefield

Life In The West

I am Bob the cowboy
As far as I go tumbleweeds blow
It's so hot in the desert, in the blazing sun
Everywhere I go I carry my gun
My horse, Dark Knight, for me is quiet
But for you always will cause a riot
With me he will fight for what's right!

Orlaith Mills (11)
Strathblane Primary School, Blanefield

What Am I?

I like hunting. I also like eating.
I am scared and shy.
I love eating birds.
I can also run very fast.
I am red and white.
I sleep during the day and I am awake at night.
I can bite very hard.
What am I?

Answer: A fox.

David Greve (8)
Strathblane Primary School, Blanefield

The Mighty Feast

Silently I hover, above the rustling trees.
Listening. Watching. Waiting.
Finally, a scuffle. A scurry.
Like a stone, I drop. Swooping, diving.
Triumphant, a meal clutched in my deathly talons.
What am I?

Answer: A buzzard.

Fin Bell (9)

Strathblane Primary School, Blanefield

Cowboy Luke

I'm a courageous and crazy cowboy
I live in the windy Wild West
Brown Betty is my bold, brave horse
Galloping gracefully and going fast
The scorching sun shines on the sand
Making Betty move magically across the land.

Gaby Spence (11)
Strathblane Primary School, Blanefield

Grookey

I like to swing from tree to tree.
Battling with my trainer.
My evolution is Thwaky and Rillaboom
I love all types of berries.
Ripe and sweet
My favourite hobby is drumming
Fun and fast.

Ellis Weaver (7)
Strathblane Primary School, Blanefield

Wild West

Vicious vultures fly around
While the west wind swirls
Scorching sun shines on the sand
As my horse hurdles heroically
Over snakes slithering sneakily about
Trying treacherously to attack.

Anna Mackinnon (10)
Strathblane Primary School, Blanefield

Trees

My leafy hair blows in the wind.
Birds land on my stick arms
My roots grow further and further every day into the soil.
I grow higher every day.

Little spiders make their webs on me.

Ruan Nicholl (8)
Strathblane Primary School, Blanefield

The Parrot

If I were a red parrot
I would see sharp leaves
And other parrots
And hear waterfalls
And I would touch the air
And eat pink worms.

AnnaBella Highett-Pavitt (6)
Wandsworth Hospital And Home Tuition PRU, London

YOUNG WRITERS INFORMATION

We hope you have enjoyed reading this book – and that you will continue to in the coming years.

If you're the parent or family member of an enthusiastic poet or story writer, do visit our website **www.youngwriters.co.uk/subscribe** and sign up to receive news, competitions, writing challenges and tips, activities and much, much more! There's lots to keep budding writers motivated!

If you would like to order further copies of this book, or any of our other titles, then please give us a call or order via your online account.

Young Writers
Remus House
Coltsfoot Drive
Peterborough
PE2 9BF
(01733) 890066
info@youngwriters.co.uk

Join in the conversation!
Tips, news, giveaways and much more!